A Warmer World

From Polar Bears to Butterflies,
How Climate Change Affects Wildlife

Caroline Arnold

Illustrated by Jamie Hogan

ini Charlesbridge

A Warming World

In 1964 a biologist working in the cloud forests of Costa Rica found a tiny toad whose bright yellow skin shone like a jewel. He named it the golden toad. Once a year, these toads came out of their burrows, mated, and laid eggs in small pools on the forest floor. After the eggs hatched, the tadpoles lived in the shallow water as they grew into toads. In the spring of 1987, the weather was unusually warm and dry. The puddles dried up soon after the eggs hatched. By the next year, almost all the toads were gone. Since 1989 no one has seen golden toads anywhere.

Golden
toad

Golden toads need the mist of the cloud forest to keep their skin moist and rain pools to hatch their eggs. As Earth has warmed, the clouds in the mountains of Costa Rica have risen higher and higher. The climate is no longer suitable for golden toads and many other animals that once thrived in the cloud forest. Golden toads are one of the first known victims of climate change.

A Changing Climate

Earth's climate has been changing for billions of years, warming and cooling many times. Recently it has been growing warmer at a faster rate than ever before. Winters are shorter, springs are earlier, and summers are hotter. In the last century, the average world temperature has risen more than one degree Fahrenheit. This may not seem like much, but a little change can make a big difference.

Climate is the average weather in a particular place measured over time. Weather is the state of the atmosphere around us at a particular place and time. In other words, climate is what you expect (for example, a wet spring) and weather is what you get (for example, a thunderstorm).

As the world has warmed, scientists have noticed many changes. Polar sea ice is shrinking and growing thinner, sea levels are rising, and patterns of rainfall are changing. Animals have responded to these changes as they search for food, shelter, and other things they need to live. In some cases, animals can adapt to new conditions. In others, their lives are threatened as their environment changes.

Polar bear

Wildlife in a Warmer World

As world temperatures rise, places that were once cool become warmer. Plants and animals can now live in places that were once too cold for them.

Arctic
fox

Foxes

Red foxes are found throughout most of the Northern Hemisphere, from the Arctic Circle to Central America and North Africa. They live mainly in forests and brushland, where they eat a wide range of prey and plant foods.

Arctic foxes are short, compact, densely furred animals that thrive in some of the coldest places on Earth. They are found mainly in the treeless regions of the Arctic. These foxes hunt birds and small mammals, and they scavenge carcasses of animals killed by larger predators.

As Earth's climate has warmed, trees and brush have begun to grow in areas of the Arctic that were once too cold for these plants. So red foxes have expanded their territory into places normally used by the smaller Arctic foxes. The Arctic foxes now have to compete with red foxes for available food.

Red fox

Escaping the Heat

As the world gets warmer, some places are becoming too hot for the plants and animals that live there. Animals can walk, fly, or swim to find a new place to live. Plants cannot move, but their seeds are carried to new locations by wind, water, and sometimes animals. If conditions are suitable the seeds may grow into new plants.

Edith's Checkerspot Butterfly

Edith's checkerspot is a small butterfly found in fields, open woods, and mountain meadows of western North America. In spring and summer females lay their eggs on the leaves of wild plants. When the eggs hatch the caterpillars eat the leaves and flowers.

In the southern and middle part of the butterflies' range, the climate has become too warm for the plants they prefer. Edith's checkerspot butterflies are disappearing from the Mexico-California border, because they can no longer find food there, while the number of butterflies is growing in British Columbia, Canada, which used to be too cold for the plants the butterflies needed.

Edith's checkerspots are also moving up mountain slopes, where warmer temperatures make it possible for the plants they prefer to grow at higher elevations. The butterflies are now found at elevations that average three hundred feet higher than they were a hundred years ago.

Higher and Cooler

As you climb up a mountain, the air becomes cooler. Each level on the mountain has its own life zone with specific kinds of plant and animal communities. As global temperatures rise, plants and animals in lower life zones may move to higher elevations. Species that live at the highest life zones have nowhere to go to find cooler temperatures.

Squirrels and Mice

In the early 1900s biologist Joseph Grinnell observed small mammals in and around California's Yosemite National Park. Recently, when scientists looked at the same species, they discovered that many of them had moved to higher elevations. The golden-mantled ground squirrel now lives about five hundred feet higher than before. For the first time, pinyon mice and pocket mice live within the park, whereas Grinnell had only found them at lower elevations. In each case, a warmer climate has made it possible for the animals to move to higher habitats.

Golden-mantled
ground squirrel

Pocket
mouse

Pinyon
mouse

Disappearing Ice

As Earth warms, the most dramatic changes are occurring in polar regions. The North Pole is in the middle of the Arctic Ocean, which is covered by a vast sheet of ice. In summer some of the ice melts; in winter it freezes again. The South Pole is in the center of Antarctica, a continent covered with large sheets of ice. These polar areas are warming faster than any other part of the world.

The light color of ice and snow reflects the sun's heat back into the atmosphere, while the dark color of land and open water absorbs the sun's heat. As ice melts, more water and land is exposed, and the temperature increases even faster than before. Scientists worry because the North Pole's ice cap has shrunk twenty percent in size since 1979. Many scientists predict that the Arctic Ocean will be ice-free in summer by 2030 or even sooner.

Scientists also worry the Antarctic ice sheets might collapse. The collapse of the West Antarctic ice sheet could raise sea levels by as much as nineteen feet. Warm ocean water has already caused huge ice shelves around the edge of the continent to break up. Polar animals depend on ice, and as the ice disappears, their lives are threatened.

Polar Bears

Polar bears are perfectly adapted to life in the Arctic. Compact bodies, dense fur coats, and a thick layer of fat help them keep warm, and their huge feet are good for swimming and walking across snow and ice. All winter long, polar bears prowl the ice in search of seals, walruses, and other marine animals. When the ice melts in spring, the polar bears go onshore. They live on their stored fat and do not hunt again until the ocean freezes in fall and they can go back on the ice.

Now that the sea ice in the Arctic is freezing later each fall and melting earlier in spring, polar bears have less time to hunt and build up fat for the summer. They are now thinner and less healthy than they were twenty years ago, and females are giving birth to fewer cubs.

Walruses

In summer, when ice melts along the Arctic coast, walruses feed on clams and crabs in the shallow water. Large chunks of ice float like islands along the shore. The walruses use this sea ice as a resting platform, pulling themselves up with their long tusks. Pups wait on the ice while their mothers dive for food. As more sea ice melts, these "islands" become fewer and farther from shore, and there are no platforms in shallow water for mothers and their pups. The pups often become separated from their mothers. They cannot survive on their own.

Penguins

As the world's climate warms, the population of penguins in Antarctica and nearby islands is changing. On the Antarctic Peninsula, once home to vast colonies of Adélie penguins, melting ice has destroyed their nests and reduced sources of food. In the last twenty-five years, the population has shrunk from forty thousand to fewer than six thousand birds. On the other hand, gentoo penguins, which previously found the Antarctic Peninsula too cold, have begun to move in. Now more than two thousand pairs of gentoos nest where the Adélies once lived.

Gentoo penguin

Adélie
penguin

Krill

Krill are small, shrimplike animals. They feed on algae, small organisms that often grow on the underside of sea ice. As temperatures rise in Antarctica, areas of sea ice have grown smaller. With less ice, there are fewer algae for the krill to feed on, so there are fewer krill. Krill is a food source for whales, seals, penguins, seabirds, squid, and fish. Without enough krill, these animals cannot live.

Changing Seasons

In a warmer world the higher temperatures of spring come earlier and the cooler temperatures of fall begin later. Patterns of rainfall and drought also change. These shifts have affected the way many animals migrate, lay eggs, hibernate, and find food.

Yellow-bellied Marmots

Marmots are large rodents often found in mountain habitats. They spend the summer eating and the winter hibernating in their burrows. Scientists studying yellow-bellied marmots in the Rocky Mountains in Colorado have found that warmer winters make the marmots wake up earlier in the spring. Forty years ago marmots typically hibernated until May. Since then the average temperatures in the area have gone up by two and one-half degrees Fahrenheit. Now the marmots wake up in April, but they cannot find the plants they normally eat. The plants will not begin to grow until the days become longer and they get more sunlight. Many marmots have starved.

Warmer Water

Water-dwelling plants and animals have also been impacted by climate change. Water in the world's oceans, lakes, and rivers is growing warmer, affecting corals, fish, and many other species.

Staghorn coral

Brain coral

Coral Reefs

Coral reefs protect shorelines from erosion by ocean waves, provide habitats and shelter for many species, and are a source of important nutrients in the food chain.

Corals are extremely sensitive and can be killed if the surrounding water becomes too cold or too hot, even by only a few degrees. When corals die, the colors disappear from their outer skeletons and leave them white, or bleached. The bleached coral can recover, but only if the water temperature returns to normal and the algae that coexist with the coral can grow again.

Coral-bleaching events have occurred more often and to a greater extent in the past twenty years than before. Global climate change may be playing a role in this increase, contributing to the destruction of major reefs and the extinction of many coral species.

Ocular coral

Plate coral

Red coral

Fish

Fish in oceans and lakes are sensitive to water temperatures. Fish such as trout and salmon prefer cool water and thrive in streams with temperatures of fifty to sixty-five degrees Fahrenheit. In many areas the fish are already living at the upper end of their temperature range, so even a small amount of warming could make streams uninhabitable. Scientists predict that trout and salmon may disappear from as much as a third of their current habitat by the year 2090 due to global warming.

On the other hand, some fish, such as largemouth bass and carp, which do well in warm water, could expand their ranges throughout the United States and Canada. If the water surface temperature goes up by four degrees, they could live four hundred miles farther north than they do now.

Trout

Carp

Bass

Salmon

25

Rising Sea Levels

As land-based ice in polar regions melts, water flows into the sea and makes the ocean higher. Sea levels are also rising because when water heats up, it expands and takes up more space. Over the last one hundred years, the world's sea level has risen about six to eight inches. By 2100 it is expected to go up three more feet.

Loggerhead Turtles

After mating in the sea, a female loggerhead turtle crawls up the beach to dig a hole in the sand and lay her eggs. Six to thirteen weeks later, the eggs hatch. With rising sea levels, the turtles' beach nesting sites may be washed away by higher tides.

Warmer temperatures are already changing the time of turtle nesting. Loggerhead turtles now lay their eggs about ten days earlier than they did fifteen years ago. With turtles the temperature of the egg in the nest determines whether the hatchlings are male or female. When the eggs are kept above eighty-six degrees Fahrenheit, most of the turtles inside grow to be females. When the eggs are kept below that temperature, the turtles become males. With rising temperatures, more females than males are being born. Without enough males, it will be harder for female turtles to find mates.

10

17

18

16

25

26

27

21

22

23

28

Earth Day

29

30

A Future Warmer World

Hundreds of species have already been affected by rising world temperatures. These animals, from tiny frogs and butterflies to polar bears and whales, show us how even small changes in temperature can produce big changes in lifestyle. Some scientists estimate that one million species are threatened with extinction because of climate change.

The world has warmed many times before. This time, however, it is warming so quickly that scientists worry plants and animals will not have time to adapt. If this happens the loss in biodiversity could be devastating.

Pollutants in Earth's atmosphere that trap the sun's heat have accelerated the pace of global warming. Learning how to control pollution can help us slow the rate of climate change, giving people and wildlife more time to adapt.

Global warming will continue to change the world in which we live. By learning how plants and animals are responding to these changes, we can better understand what to expect in a future warmer world.

Arctic fox

Glossary

algae: small plants that grow in rivers, lakes, and oceans

Arctic: the area between the Arctic Circle and the North Pole

Arctic Circle: the imaginary line parallel to the equator, about 1,650 miles from the North Pole

biodiversity: the number and variety of living things found within a geographic region

climate: the average weather in a place measured over time

cloud forest: a tropical forest that has almost constant cloud cover, even during the dry season

coral reef: an ocean mound composed of the skeletons of living coral together with minerals and other matter

elevation: the distance above sea level

food chain: the feeding relationships in a community in which each member feeds on the one below it, with the largest predators at the top of the chain

habitat: the place and conditions in which a plant or animal lives

hibernate: to pass the winter in a long, deep sleep. When animals hibernate, their bodies' processes slow down.

life zone: an area with plant and animal communities similar to those found elsewhere at the same altitude and latitude

migrate: to move to another location with the seasons

rodent: a gnawing animal with a pair of chisel-shaped teeth at the front of its upper and lower jaw

weather: the condition of the air at a particular place and time

For More Information

Websites

**Ecosystems and Biodiversity—Animals—
Environmenal Protection Agency**
http://epa.gov/climatechange/effects/
eco_animals.html

**Effects on Wildlife and Habitat—
National Wildlife Federation**
http://www.nwf.org/Global-Warming/
Effects-on-Wildlife-and-Habitat.aspx

**Warming Creating Extinction Risks for Hibernating—
National Geographic**
http://news.nationalgeographic.com/news/2008/02/
080201-hibernation_2.html

Books

Cherry, Lynne, and Gary Braasch. *How We Know What We Know About Our Changing Climate: Scientists and Kids Explore Global Warming.* Nevada City, CA: Dawn Publications, 2008.

David, Laurie, and Cambria Gordon. *The Down-to-Earth Guide to Global Warming.* New York: Orchard Books, 2007.

Gore, Al. *An Inconvenient Truth: The Crisis of Global Warming.* New York: Viking Children's Books, 2007.

Simon, Seymour. *Global Warming.* New York: Collins, 2010.

For Alessandra, Lucas,
and Paige—C. A.

For Mum—J. H.

Published by Charlesbridge
85 Main Street
Watertown, MA 02472
(617) 926-0329
www.charlesbridge.com

Library of Congress Cataloging-in-Publication Data
Arnold, Caroline.
    A warmer world : from polar bears to butterflies, how climate
change affects wildlife / Caroline Arnold ; illustrated by Jamie Hogan.
        p. cm.
    ISBN 978-1-58089-266-7 (reinforced for library use)
    ISBN 978-1-58089-267-4 (softcover)
1. Global warming—Juvenile literature. 2. Climatic changes—
Juvenile literature. I. Hogan, Jamie. II. Title.
QC981.8.G56A76 2012
363.738'74—dc22   2011000811

Printed in China
(hc)   10 9 8 7 6 5 4 3 2 1
(sc)   10 9 8 7 6 5 4 3 2 1

Illustrations done in charcoal pencil and pastel on sanded
    paper with elements of collage, paper, and tags
Display type and text type set in Minya Nouvelle,
    Triplex, and Janson
Color separations by KHL Chroma Graphics,
    Singapore
Manufactured by Regent Publishing Services,
    Hong Kong
Printed September 2011 in Shenzhen,
    Guangdong, China
Production supervision by Brian G. Walker
Designed by Whitney Leader-Picone